A Self-Administered Poison
The System and Functions of Soviet Censorship

D1567776

THE EUROPEAN HUMANITIES RESEARCH CENTRE

UNIVERSITY OF OXFORD

Director: Martin McLaughlin
Fiat-Serena Professor of Italian Studies

The European Humanities Research Centre of the University of Oxford organizes a range of academic activities, including conferences and workshops, and publishes scholarly works under its own imprint, LEGENDA. Within Oxford, the EHRC bridges, at the research level, the main humanities faculties: Modern Languages, English, Modern History, Classics and Philosophy, Music and Theology. The Centre stimulates interdisciplinary research collaboration throughout these subject areas and provides an Oxford base for advanced researchers in the humanities.

The Centre's publications programme focuses on making available the results of advanced research in medieval and modern languages and related interdisciplinary areas. An Editorial Board, whose members are drawn from across the British university system, covers the principal European languages. Titles currently include works on Arabic, Catalan, Chinese, English, French, German, Italian, Portuguese, Russian, Spanish, Greek and Yiddish literature. In addition, the EHRC co-publishes with the Society for French Studies, the Modern Humanities Research Association and the British Comparative Literature Association. The Centre also publishes a Special Lecture Series under the LEGENDA imprint, and a journal, *Oxford German Studies*.

Further information:
Kareni Bannister, Senior Publications Officer
European Humanities Research Centre
University of Oxford
76 Woodstock Road, Oxford OX2 6LE
enquiries@ehrc.ox.ac.uk
www.ehrc.ox.ac.uk

LEGENDA EDITORIAL BOARD

Chairman
Professor Martin McLaughlin, Magdalen College

Editorial Adviser
Professor Malcolm Bowie, Christ's College, Cambridge

Professor Ian Maclean, All Souls College (French)
Professor Marian Hobson Jeanneret, Queen Mary University of London
(French)
Professor Ritchie Robertson, St John's College (German)
Professor Lesley Sharpe, University of Exeter (German)
Dr Diego Zancani, Balliol College (Italian)
Professor David Robey, University of Reading (Italian)
Dr Stephen Parkinson, Linacre College (Portuguese)
Professor Helder Macedo, King's College London (Portuguese)
Professor Gerald Smith, New College (Russian)
Professor David Shepherd, University of Sheffield (Russian)
Dr David Pattison, Magdalen College (Spanish)
Dr Alison Sinclair, Clare College, Cambridge (Spanish)
Professor Martin Maiden, Trinity College (Linguistics)
Professor Peter Matthews, St John's College, Cambridge (Linguistics)
Dr Elinor Shaffer, School of Advanced Study, London
(Comparative Literature)
Professor Colin Davis, University of Warwick
(Modern Literature, Film and Theory)

Senior Publications Officer
Kareni Bannister

Publications Officer
Dr Graham Nelson

LEGENDA

European Humanities Research Centre
Special Lecture Series

This series publishes a selection of public lectures in the Humanities
given at the University of Oxford and was established to mark the
150th anniversary of the Taylor Institution.

Previously published in this series:

1. *Proust: Questions d'identité*
by Julia Kristeva

2. *History Painting and Narrative*
by Peter Brooks

3. *L'écriture testamentaire à la fin du Moyen Age: Identité, dispersion, trace*
by Jacqueline Cerquiglini-Toulet

4. *Le partage de la parole*
by Luce Irigaray

A Self-Administered Poison

The System and Functions of Soviet Censorship

ARLEN BLYUM

TRANSLATED BY I. P. FOOTE

GUELPH HUMBER LIBRARY
205 Humber College Blvd
Toronto, ON   M9W 5L7

LEGENDA

European Humanities Research Centre
University of Oxford
Special Lecture Series 5
2003

Published by the
European Humanities Research Centre
of the University of Oxford
47 Wellington Square
Oxford OX1 2JF

LEGENDA is the publications imprint of the
European Humanities Research Centre

ISBN 1 900755 76 9
ISSN 1466–8165

First published 2003

All rights reserved. No part of this publication may be reproduced or disseminated or
transmitted in any form or by any means, electronic, mechanical, photocopying,
recording or otherwise, or stored in any retrieval system, or otherwise used in any
manner whatsoever without the express permission of the copyright owner

British Library Cataloguing in Publication Data
A CIP catalogue record for this book is available from the British Library

English translation © European Humanities Research Centre of the
University of Oxford 2003

LEGENDA series designed by Cox Design Partnership, Witney, Oxon
Printed in Great Britain by
Information Press
Eynsham
Oxford OX8 1JJ

Chief Copy-Editor: Genevieve Hawkins

Arlen Viktorovich Blyum was born in 1933. He has worked for many years as a Professor in the St Petersburg State Institute of Culture, where his teaching and research have been concerned with the history of the book, a field in which he is one of Russia's leading authorities. In recent years he has done notable pioneering work in investigating the archives of *Glavlit*, the body which effectively controlled all publishing activity in the Soviet Union from the 1920s until the collapse of the regime. He has written extensively on the book and censorship. His recent publications include three books based on his archival researches, *Za kulisami 'Ministerstva Pravdy': tainaya istoriya sovetskoi tsenzury, 1917–1929* (St Petersburg, 1994), *Sovetskaya tsenzura v epokhu total'nogo terrora: 1929–1953* (St Petersburg, 2000) and *Zensur in der UdSSR: Archivdokumente, 1917–1991* (Bochum, 1999). These provide the first detailed account of censorship under the Soviets; another work is in preparation.

The English translation of this lecture is by I. P. Foote, Emeritus Fellow of the Queen's College, Oxford.

The Ilchester Lectures are funded by a bequest to the University by William Thomas Horner Fox-Strangways, fourth Earl of Ilchester, to support the study of the Slavonic languages, literatures, and history (see J. S. G. Simmons, 'Slavonic Studies at Oxford, 1844–1909', *Oxford Slavonic Papers*, N.S. 13 (1980), 1–27). They started in 1870 and have been delivered by a wide range of distinguished scholars and writers, including the first Professor of Russian and other Slavonic languages at Oxford, W. R. Morfill (1870–3, 1883), Konstantin Bal'mont (1897), Nikolay Berdyaev (1947), C. M. Bowra (1949), Lord David Cecil (1960), V. S. Pritchett (1960), Roman Jakobson (1950, 1963), M. P. Alekseev (1963), D. S. Likhachev (1967, 1987), Ya. S. Lur'e (1988). A number of the lectures have been published in *Oxford Slavonic Papers*.

A Self-Administered Poison: The System and Functions of Soviet Censorship

Censorship is one of the most important mechanisms for the defence of ideological and political systems. By their control of the sources of information the censors ensure, or at least think they ensure, the optimal functioning of the system which they defend. Censorship has existed as long as books have been written, though, of course, it became institutionalized only after the invention of printing, which demanded particular means and methods of control. In different societies, depending on their structure, censorship took different forms: in some it was reduced to a minimum, in others it flourished (if the word is appropriate in this context). Godunov-Cherdyntsev, the poet-hero of Nabokov's novel *Dar* (*The Gift*), reflects that 'In Russia the censorship department arose before literature; its fateful seniority has been always in evidence'.[1]

Some form of censorship has existed and does exist in all societies: what counts is its nature and the intensity of its operation. As well as from the state, measures to restrict the freedom of the printed word can come from social, financial, and other institutions. In the case of the state, we are concerned with administrative censorship, pre-liminary and punitive, which removes layers of a text—the first before publication, the second after. In other cases, we are concerned with schools of thought, critical attitudes, and the press, which accord to a text a particular status and aura, causing it either to be blessed and sanctified by public opinion or, on the contrary, to be condemned and cut off from particular, if not all, sections of the reading public.

It has long been noted that the very concept of 'censorship', seen, on the one hand, as an institution of government, or, on the other, as a system of quasi-legal regulations whose function is to control the printed word and the means of exerting influence on it, does not remotely cover or even approximately convey the meaning it acquires under totalitarian regimes, the Soviet regime in particular. In such regimes censorship is a phenomenon of an entirely different order, of a kind that has never existed in any place or at any time before: for that reason the very word 'censorship' is often used not in its strict sense, but is applied by extension to *any* means of restraint on freedom of speech. However, this concept, with its many aspects and meanings, is difficult to define in any precise sense, and it is best to consider it in its first and basic meaning, since the subject will otherwise become too broad to allow clear definition. It should, however, be borne in mind that in the Soviet context censorship itself, as a powerful institution of the state, and the means and methods it employed to influence the printed word, in no way exhausted the available means of pressure and regulation, and, in certain cases and at particular stages of Soviet history, played a much less significant role than the actions of the Party-ideological establishment.

In the strict sense of the word censorship should still be taken to mean the control by the state of the content, publication, and distribution of printed texts. In totalitarian states its main characteristic and the basis on which it exists is found not in published laws, but in secret instructions issued by the ideological hierarchy and in the establishment of a special institution not answerable to public opinion. In the present account I shall consider censorship chiefly from this viewpoint, focusing on three aspects of this immense and many-faceted phenomenon: I shall first characterize the hierarchic, strictly graduated system of Soviet censorship that had come into being by the end of the 1920s; secondly, reveal what basic functions it fulfilled; and, thirdly, assess the results and effectiveness of its operation.

In the last ten years Russian and foreign historians and literary scholars (among them the present author) have collected and analysed, if not in full, a large amount of previously secret documentary material,[2] which enables us to draw certain conclusions and make some general observations.

By the late 1920s a many-tiered control mechanism had developed; this was *Glavlit*,[3] the main component part of the 'Ministry of Truth' (Orwell's term, in his great novel *Nineteen Eighty-Four*, for the state institution of thought-control—an institution remarkably similar, even in its details, to its Soviet counterpart). In time, an all-pervasive control of the printed and publicly spoken word was created. This complex structure had at least five levels or filters, and a text, as it rose through these different levels, could suffer serious deformation or simply not appear in print. I will mention only in passing that mysterious process of the subconscious which has been recognized in classical psychoanalysis and is also termed 'censorship'. Freud regularly uses the term to describe the 'testing agency' which controls the passage of ideas from the unconscious to the conscious: 'There is a force in the mind which exercises the functions of a censorship, and which excludes from consciousness and from any influence on action all tendencies which displease it'.[4] Freud, incidentally, in using the word 'censorship' for this psychological process, more than once referred it specifically to Russia, illustrating its function by describing the way foreign publications were treated by censors at the Russian frontier—for example, in a letter of 1897 he wrote: 'Have you ever seen a foreign newspaper which passed Russian censorship at the frontier? Words, whole clauses and sentences are blacked out so that the rest becomes unintelligible. A *Russian censorship* of this kind comes about in psychoses and produces the apparently meaningless *deliria*.'[5]

As it increased in scope and rigour, the system of Soviet censorship took on the form of a pyramid. First, at the base of the pyramid, was *self-censorship* (other terms: autocensorship, inner censorship, inner editor, inner censor), that is, self-imposed limitation in the creation or dissemination of a work by which the author accommodates himself to particular taboos imposed either by the state, society, the reading public, or by his own aesthetic taste and moral principles. Inner censorship can be regarded, in certain, relatively rare, individual cases, as a kind of defence mechanism that served to protect the author and prevent him falling foul of the regular censorship or other—for him even more dangerous—organs of the state. In such cases, the author seeks to uphold his creative freedom and, harbouring no illusions, writes 'in full voice', heedless of censorship conditions and fully aware that his work is 'for the drawer' with no hope of appearing in print (for instance, a number of works by Andrei Platonov, Anna Akhmatova's *Requiem*, many poems by Mandel'shtam, Bulgakov's *Master and Margarita*, and the 'grown-up' works of the *avant-garde* OBERIU (*Ob″edinenie real′nogo iskusstva*).

The second and main variety of self-censorship, particularly in totalitarian societies, occurs much more frequently and takes the form of a purely conformist adaptation on the part of the author to the existing circumstances and the 'rules of the game'. The overwhelming majority of authors gave in and learned the technique of survival: they mastered the art of the sack-race, running, though, not in one but in several sacks at the same time. In the Soviet period self-censorship involved the author in seeking to guess what ideological, political, moral, aesthetic and other objections his text might encounter in the course of its progress through the official instances of control (Party-ideological circles, state censorship, publishing bodies, etc.). Sometimes he succeeded, sometimes, despite his efforts, he failed, since he could not bring himself, in Mayakovsky's phrase, 'to step on the throat of his own song'[6] or was insufficiently aware of 'which way the wind was blowing'. From the 1930s self-censorship gradually became second nature to the great majority of authors, with dire effects on their work. Continuous mimicry leads inevitably to the deformation and loss of talent. The inner censor becomes inseparable from the external censor, and often the first proves stricter than the second. Through constant self-censorship a writer dries up, loses his originality, and in his efforts 'not to stand out' and 'to be like everyone else' he becomes cynical, concerned only with getting himself into print come what may (this happened in the case of some major authors who had made a brilliant start to their writing careers in the 1920s—notable examples are Yury Olesha and Valentin Kataev).

Self-censorship became the basic factor in the creative process, to the extent that in the view of some scholars the administrative control of literature and art by the state was, in practice, superfluous. According to E. Dobrenko, 'socialist realism is not regulated, but *self-regulated* art, it is not control, but *self-control*: for the Soviet writer there can be no 'censorship problem', for as the process of censoring turns from being a part of the Soviet writer's 'act of creation' into an external problem (or, more than a problem, an obstacle), so he [the author] ceases to be a *Soviet* writer in the direct sense of the word... The Soviet writer had no stricter censor than himself: he *was* the censor.' Dobrenko makes a general point about the development of literature in Soviet society: '*The conversion of the author into his own censor—that is the true history of Soviet literature*' and dismisses as 'trivial' the 'sovietological' (with negative connotation) claim of the 'terror against creative artists' that reigned in the Soviet era.[7]

It seems to me that Dobrenko goes too far: if one accepts his view, it becomes incomprehensible why, from time to time, the authorities found it necessary to go into 'ideological convulsions' (as Dostoevsky puts it in *The Devils*), calling to heel authors who had stepped out of line and creating an atmosphere of terror. Of course, there were intervals when the actual control by *Glavlit* was no more than a purely formal monitoring operation to prevent the publication of military secrets, but the very existence of this institution was a menace and sufficient in itself, whatever its actual function in the literary process.

As Anna Akhmatova wrote in one of her poems of 1921:

> А в пещере у дракона
> Нет пощады, нет закона,
> И висит на стенке плеть
> Чтобы песен мне не петь.[8]

[And in the cavern of the dragon
There is no mercy and no law,
And on the wall there hangs a whip
That I may not sing my songs.]

The second level of censorship was editorial censorship, carried out by operatives in publishing houses, journals, newspapers, television and radio stations, theatres, and so on. With good reason Nadezhda Mandel'shtam reckoned that for the writer an editor was more to be feared than a censor: 'In our country everyone knows that it is not the censor who emasculates a book—he only applies the finishing touches —but the editor who zealously digs his teeth into a text and chews over its every last detail.'[9]

The directors of publishing houses, appointed from the upper echelons of the Party, and their editors, risen from its ranks, subjected texts to severe ideological purging, in doing which they yielded nothing to the actual organs of censorship, occasionally surpassing them in their zeal. At this level too a fateful and malign part was played by the heads and functionaries of the so-called 'creative unions' —of writers, composers, artists, etc.—which exercised control over the institutions and activities in their charge—publishing houses, exhibitions, theatrical performances, etc. By the 1940s-1950s editors had as a rule supplanted the censors, for the most part leaving to them only the protection of the 'Military-economic schedule of restricted information'. In fairness, it must be said that among editors there were a number of talented and concerned individuals who exerted themselves to resist these ideological and political dictates: A. K. Voronsky in *Krasnaya nov'* in the 1920s,[10] the 'Marshak group' in Lendetizdat (*Leningradskoe detskoe izdatel'stvo*) in the 1930s which was suppressed before the end of the decade,[11] A. T. Tvardovsky and his colleagues in *Novyi mir* in the 'Thaw' of the 1960s,[12] and others. However, with the passage of time a new generation of Soviet editors was trained, who formed a united front with the censors and waged war against authors—with the editors often in the vanguard. Being more educated than the censors, they posed a greater danger for writers, noting things which the censors would overlook (for instance, 'covert citation' of forbidden texts, undesirable allusions). Editors were extremely careful to check that the text would not give rise to any so-called 'instinctive associations', or dangerous and undesirable comparisons, although they were not always successful. From the 1940s a text so edited hardly ever met with objections from the censors, except for chance infringements of the regulation on 'military secrets'. Editors' suspicions were above all directed at the sub-text of a work, produced by the use of 'Aesopic' language and various devices of 'making the V-sign in your pocket', etc. In the Russian, and particularly the Soviet, conditions of censorship, 'reading between the lines' through the course of a text, the ability to discover the hidden, inner, second sense of a work and interpret it has always been an essential feature of the shared creativity of the writer and the reader. The author addresses his 'reader-friend', counting on him to participate in the creative process and conjure up parallels relevant to the realities of Soviet life.[13]

As time went on, given the operation of self-censorship already described, the methods employed by editors to interfere with a text became ever more refined. Editors and internal referees, as Yury Trifonov caustically observed, 'filtered ten times water that was already distilled'.[14] This was understandable enough: each of them was justifying his existence, and if they had not carried out their function, the whole establishment of editors and referees would have been superfluous. Each line was scrupulously examined, and the text was subjected not only to the excision of 'inconvenient parts', but also to substantial changes and, not infrequently, to censors' additions. For this reason, none (or practically none) of the texts published in Soviet conditions can be considered authentic or in full accord with the will and original idea of the author. Every text is a collective product, with the state as one of its collective authors.

Traditionally, and not only in Soviet society, there is another kind of editorial 'censorship'. This is the so-called 'journal censorship' that manifests itself when a journal's contributors, like-minded and united (on the principle of 'for us or against us'), its style and manner of presentation, and, above all, its ideology are chosen—within, of course, permitted and very restricted limits—by the editorial body.[15] However, unlike the 1920s and the later periods of 'thaw' and 'stagnation', in the 'classical' Soviet period (the 1930s–1940s) the conditions of censorship terror made it impossible to continue this tradition. Apart from some insignificant nuances, the literary journals of the time lost their individuality of style and, more particularly, of ideology.

Although not the sole guardian of the printed word, *Glavlit* played the key role, since it and its local agencies carried out all the practical work. One should not, as some do, underestimate the part played by the veritable army of *Glavlit* censors. First, much depended on their decisions, and secondly, it was they who passed on to higher authority any material involving 'anti-Soviet' or 'wrecking' intrigues and tendencies in literature and the media in general, which in turn gave rise to still tougher ideological demands. In the atmosphere of fear then reigning this was a spiralling process analogous to that which operates in the mass extermination of people.

The *Glavlit* censorship occupied the middle place in the five-tier system of control of the press and the spoken (at least, publicly spoken) word: below it the filters provided by authors and editors, above it the directives of the police and the Party, which it rigorously carried out. The end product of this graduated filtration was to be a fully distilled text that conformed in every respect to the aims and intentions of the authorities. Without *Glavlit* as an institute of state administration, the system could not have functioned efficiently. To it was entrusted the task of eliminating everything which in the least degree ran counter to the latest ideological directives.

The fourth level of censorship was the 'punitive' censorship exercised by the organs of the secret political police—called variously during this time the OGPU/NKVD/NKGB/MGB, whose structure included a Department of Political Control (later replaced by the Fifth Directorate of the KGB).[16] It should be noted that the term 'punitive censorship' is now most commonly used with reference to the judicial censorship, adopted in many democratic states (and, indeed, in Russia after the 1905 Revolution), where no sanctions can be imposed on a publication except by decision of a court of law. Here, however, the term is used in its original sense and means punishment without recourse to the courts and—in order to detect punishable offences— the maintenance of a clandestine surveillance both of the current course of literature and of works already published. At different stages the part played by these organs varied in its importance. In the 1920s, when the *Glavlit* system was beginning to develop, they were essentially superior censorship bodies which required the submission of most published works for further scrutiny and which checked them for errors made by the regular personnel of *Glavlit* itself. Though formally coming within the structure of *Narkompros* (*Narodnyi komissariat prosveshcheniya*), *Glavlit*, in fact, was subordinated not to it, but to the state security services, of which it was a kind of affiliate.

In the 1930s, when the personnel of the censorship organs had been selected, reinforced with proven communists, and appropriately trained, the political-control function of the OGPU/NKVD did not decrease; but it did take on a somewhat different character. Although the two institutions worked hand in hand, from the 1930s there was a division between their spheres of influence and competence. *Glavlit* stood by its 'sacred right' to allow (or prevent) the publication of any work, whatever the publishing body, including even publications of the organs of state security. Maintaining the appearance of 'legality', the latter, from the 1940s, turned to *Glavlit*, as expert witness, for evidence in cases where it was necessary to prove a 'fact of anti-Soviet propaganda' (a term boundless in its interpretation) in books discovered in searches, imported from abroad, etc. To judge by the documents,[17] *Glavlit* provided its decisions on the principle of 'What is it you'd like?', discovering such 'facts' in practically any publication.

It is difficult to define the line dividing the spheres of activity of the organs of censorship and state security. In 1952 the Party Central Committee considered a project by which *Glavlit* and all its associated agencies would be transferred to the MGB,[18] but in the confusion which followed the death of Stalin it was set aside; however, for a period in 1953 *Glavlit* came under the authority of the MVD (*Ministerstvo vnutrennikh del*).

The next, fifth, level of control was at the top of the pyramid—the Agitprop department (Department of Agitation and Propaganda) of the Party Central Committee. It was in the charge of the Secretary for Ideology, who, as a rule, was the second man in the Party hierarchy. The Agitprop had the first and final, deciding, word in determining the fate of authors and their works, as well as of publishing houses, journals, newspapers, and other means of information; it issued 'directives' (*ustanovki*) which were rigorously carried out by *Glavlit*. At this level censorship operated by means of what in Party jargon was termed 'decision taking' by the ideological agencies of the Party, principally the departments and directorates within the Central Committee which in different years went under different names: Agitprop, Kul'tprop,[19] *Upravlenie propagandy i agitatsii*, *Ideologicheskii otdel*[20] and others. Initially, they held back from open acknowledgement of their censorship functions and, when necessary, sought refuge behind some 'Soviet pseudonym', issuing their directives in the name of *Narkompros, Gosizdat, Glavpolitprosvet*,[21] and other 'legitimate' Soviet organizations. Subsequently, the need for such disguise was no longer felt.

Above the organizational pyramid stood the supreme figure of the Party General Secretary, the dictator himself, who was the ultimate arbiter and whose verdict was beyond appeal. From his will and whim hung the fate of works by literary writers, scholars, and authors of all kinds, as indeed did their very lives. The intervention of the General Secretary reached its apogee during the dictatorship of Stalin, who unfortunately took a keen interest in literature. He could play cat-and-mouse with this or that author (as he did, for instance, with Pasternak and Bulgakov), give the order to 'preserve' them but not publish their works, write on a book by Andrey Platonov the single word 'Swine', and so forth.[22] On occasion, for pragmatic purposes the General Secretary could play the role of the sovereign, correcting the excesses of his too zealous officials—following in this the example of Nicholas I who allowed the performance on stage of Gogol''s *The Inspector General* and the publication of his *Dead Souls*, which the Moscow censors had banned. Such unexpected acts inspired in some authors a mystical faith in Stalin's 'wisdom' and 'justice'—which may well have been his intention when, in similar cases, he acted this way.

In speaking of these different levels of control, one should not see the whole process as something purely mechanical, in which the passage of a text from the author to higher levels takes place in strict hierarchical order. In practice, the activities of the various institutions and instances we have mentioned were curiously intermeshed, and it is impossible to draw a clear line between them. Besides this, a very active role in the process was played by 'volunteer' censors who alerted the competent authorities to ideological 'lapses' made not only by authors and editors, but also by the censors themselves. Always slightly 'ahead of progress' were certain literary critics,[23] whose reviews, both in style and in content, differed little from actual censors' reports; indeed, their vigilance quite often went beyond what had been decided by *Glavlit*. Where the different branches of ideological surveillance are indivisible and sometimes indistinguishable in their functions, one is confronted with one of the major characteristics of the totalitarian state.

In totalitarian and rigorous police-states the functions of censorship are many and varied. By my count, there are a good ten such functions: repressive, regulatory, model-setting, ideological, selective, protective, etc. The repressive function, for instance, is fulfilled by the operation of a rigorous censorship, unfettered by law and based solely on so-called 'revolutionary legality and expediency'; at the disposition of the Soviet censorship and related organs of repression was a whole range of punitive measures which could be taken against authors, producers, distributors, readers, and anyone in possession of undesirable information. The regulatory function was to establish and maintain control over the production and distribution of information resources. The rules of control should be determined by law, but even when there were laws, they had no operative value, since in practice matters were most often determined by secret instructions, recommendations, directives, circulars, and so on. The purpose of the model-setting function was to fix certain texts in a 'model', canonical form in which they became more or less holy writ, and also to sanction particular styles of artistic production and academic schools of thought (in Soviet conditions there was only one style—socialist realism, and only one school of thought—Marxism).

A number of these functions are characteristic of the censorship policy of pre-revolutionary Russia and of other states. Within the limits of this article I shall, though, refer only to those prime functions which are the most characteristic of, and specific to, totalitarian regimes as exemplified by the Soviet Union.

Of these the most important is, of course, the ideological function, which permeates all the others. Its purpose was to force people to have the exclusively 'correct' ideas about the world, to form the man equipped with the one and only true *Weltanschauung*. The Soviet state gradually came to be dominated not so much by an ideocracy as by a logocracy—the power of words. Towards the end of the regime few people had any concern for the purity of the moribund ideology; what mattered was to write and say the necessary words, to maintain some kind of ideological decorum. This may be the reason for the rapid and relatively bloodless collapse of the regime, based as it was on words alone. The main function of ideological censorship was to create a phantom, unreal world, the product, on the one hand, of hallucinations (when a man sees what is not there in reality), and, on the other hand, so-called negative hallucinations (when a man is so brainwashed by propaganda that he fails to see or be aware of reality). It is not even, as is commonly claimed, a matter of concealing the truth, but of creating by all the means of propaganda what Jeffrey Brooks calls 'a stylized, ritualistic, and internally consistent public culture that became its own reality and supplanted other forms of public reflection and expression'.[24]

Propaganda acts like a self-administered poison—a total toxication of the social organism sets in, which leads to its end. The malign constancy and repetitiveness of Russian history clearly left their stamp on the particular features of the ideocratic regime and its leading-rein, which the universal and all-pervading censorship came to be. It follows the law of the pendulum which cannot depart from its defined course and swings from terror to thaw through a phase of stagnation—and back again to terror.[25] But once this pendulum law is broken, once power departs from its defined course, not in the direction of terror, which, as the history of our country has shown, can be boundless, but too far in the direction of thaw and liberalization, then the regime is done for. This was what happened at the end of the 1980s when the regime was swept away by the freedom of expression that came with the declaration of *glasnost'*.

Integrally bound up with the ideological function is the selective function. Although as a term 'selection' relates to the natural sciences, indicating the processes of selection and development which produce new species and hybrids of plants and animals, it can be used metaphorically in respect of the basic functions of censorship control. The new experts in selection—disciples of Michurin and Lysenko in the field of ideology—were also concerned with the selective process in its application to cultural values, choosing not the best, but the worst or, at any rate, nothing above the average and mediocre. Essential components in the 'reforging' of minds were the re-writing of history and the decisive changes and unprecedented restrictions in the repertoire of reading. (Incidentally, the very word 'reforging' has an ominous sense which those who coined the term failed to notice: on the evidence of Dostoevsky's *Notes from the House of the Dead*, it was the term used for the replacement of the fetters worn by a convict in transit to Siberia by the fetters he would wear when put to work after his arrival.[26] There was no 'falling of fetters' in Soviet times, the fetters were simply made heavier.)

For three-quarters of a century an attempt was made to breed a new species of human being, profoundly ignorant in all aspects of life, an infantile individual of life-long immaturity and distorted mind— ideal material from which to create the 'new society'. Pursuing a deliberate policy of negative selection or, as Solzhenitsyn put it, the 'selective *anti-selection*, choosing for destruction everything that was striking or distinctive and better than average...',[27] the authorities sought to uproot anything that stood out and was 'above the peasant boot'. Using censorship as a formative agent in this process, the regime sought to bring society into a state of cultural uniformity and mediocrity. This policy of cultural levelling was carried out by 'positive' as well as by punitive measures. On the one hand, cultural advance was promoted by the elimination of illiteracy, universal education, and books published in runs of millions, while, on the other, unprecedented restrictions were imposed by censorship— together, these measures were intended to create a uniform society. The cultural 'heights' and the democratic 'depths' were simultaneously removed. At this time there was no place for the élite literature of the aristocracy and the experimental writing of the *avant-garde*, nor, equally, for the crude coloured prints the common folk bought at the fair. The popular print received, of course, new form in the primitive works of propaganda—more literate, more 'correct', but lacking in the characteristic charm of the original.

A new culture of mediocrity was created as far removed from the heights as from the depths. Ruled out, on the one hand, were Stravinsky, Schoenberg, much of Shostakovich, one of whose works the formalists had denounced as 'chaos instead of music';[28] so too, on the other, were the street organ-grinder, the leisurely light-hearted lyrics of the cabaret, and jazz: cultural contrasts were artificially levelled out and effaced. Authors who have written about the reasons for the notorious Central Committee directive on *Zvezda* and *Leningrad* in August 1946[29] have offered several versions of why two such diverse writers as Zoshchenko and Akhmatova should be lumped together and become victims of this literary pogrom. In the case of Zoshchenko, the author himself thought that Stalin harboured a grudge against him because he had recognized himself in the rough-spoken man with the moustache in one of his pre-war stories, 'Lenin and the Sentry' ('Lenin i chasovoi').[30] In it a young worker on guard at Smol'ny in 1917, not knowing Lenin by sight, asks him for his pass. In the original version the sentry was given a rude dressing-down by a person with a small beard and a moustache. The censor had the notion that it was aimed at Kalinin and advised removing the beard. The second redaction had the rough-spoken man with a moustache, but no beard, which was worse still since it created an association with Stalin himself ('whiskered Daddy', as he was called in the labour-camps). The moustache had to be removed as well: in subsequent editions, even those published today, the character is merely 'some person, probably one of the office-staff' with no sign whatever of any growth on his face. So the man's face was gradually depilated in order not to suggest any inappropriate associations.[31]

This curious and, in itself, noteworthy explanation does not, though, lie at the heart of the matter. It was not by chance that such different writers were coupled together as the principal targets in this purge of ideas. In the eyes of the Party leadership, Akhmatova belonged to the 'heights', writing refined 'aesthete's' poetry for the high-brows; Zoshchenko, enormously popular with the ordinary people, belonged to the 'depths'—there was no need for either of them.

In practice, the selective function of censorship was fulfilled in the deliberate and planned destruction of whole layers of literary culture. In the very early days of the Soviet regime, in 1922, a purging of so-called 'counter-revolutionary' literature from the libraries was initiated, carried out by *Glavpolitprosvet*, which was headed at the time by Lenin's wife N. N. Krupskaya. At the same time in libraries enormous *spetskhrany* (special closed collections) were created in which tens and hundreds of thousands of books and periodicals were buried away.

In cultural terms the so-called 'first echelon' of Bolshevik leaders differed distinctly from the second. Although the aesthetic tastes of Lenin and his wife were simple, not to say primitive, the Leader did, nonetheless, entrust the finer points of cultural policy to a man of culture, A. V. Lunacharsky, the Commissar for Education. Among Lunacharsky's inner circle were 'enlightened Bolsheviks', critics and editors, such as A. K. Voronsky, the editor of *Krasnaya nov'*, and N. S. Angarsky,[32] a supporter of Bulgakov, who, with a number of others, did much for the development of literature in the 1920s. It was their view that everything in the cultural 'economy' could be of use; all that was needed was to 'educate and re-educate' the artists and writers and put their talents at the service of the new ideology. The range of prohibitions was, however, vastly extended in the 1930s, with the result that for the new, 'second echelon' of Party leaders who were building a totalitarian society, much in culture was simply incomprehensible—and therefore dangerous. The jocular, but in fact perfectly accurate definition of socialist realism as 'Singing praises to the authorities in a form they can understand' had a point.

The policy of mass 'bibliocide' that was carried on over several decades is fully in accord with the formulations contained in the Party slogans of Big Brother in Orwell's *Nineteen Eighty-Four*. 'Ignorance is Strength' and 'Who controls the past controls the future; who controls the present controls the past'. In the same novel Orwell wrote: 'If the Party could thrust its hand into the past and say of this or that event, *it never happened*, that, surely, was more terrifying than mere torture or death.'[33]

The language itself, like the celebrated 'Newspeak' of *Nineteen Eighty-Four*, offers prime evidence as to the nature and point of the censorship repressions. What, for instance, is meant by the prescription that, in purging public libraries of pre-revolutionary editions, only the 'least unacceptable' should be left? And there is the astonishing expression encountered in censorship documents—'slanderous fact': it is recognized that the fact exists, but reference to it is a slander. The question is simply: whose interests does the fact serve?

A no less characteristic function of the Soviet censorship, unique of its kind, was the prescriptive (or 'imperative') function. If the functions previously mentioned are to a greater or lesser degree present in the censorship systems of other strictly ordered police states, the prescriptive function appears to be an invention of the communist regime. At any rate, it was the communist regime which required its censors not only to forbid works that ran counter to the aims and intentions of its political and ideological programme, but also to 'educate' authors by prescribing what and how they should write. This was well put by V. V. Nabokov in a lecture he delivered at Cornell University in 1958 on 'Writers, Censorship, and Readers in Russia'. Harbouring no romantic illusions about the supposed beneficent conditions in which literature and the press functioned in pre-revolutionary Russia (illusions shared by certain émigrés and maintained by some even in Russia today), Nabokov did nonetheless indicate the fundamental difference between the old and the new censorship: '[in the past] books and writers may be banned and banished, censors might be rogues and fools, be-whiskered Tsars might stamp and storm; but that wonderful discovery of Soviet times, the method of making the entire literary corporation write what the state deems fit—this method was unknown in old Russia, although no doubt many a reactionary statesman hoped to find such a tool... In Russia before the Soviet rule there did exist restrictions, but no orders were given to artists. They were—those nineteenth-century writers, composers, and painters—quite certain that they lived in a country of oppression and slavery, but they had something which one can appreciate only now, namely, the immense advantage over their grandsons in modern Russia of not being compelled to say that there was no oppression and no slavery.'[34]

In short, in the past censorship could only prohibit, in the Soviet era it could both prohibit and prescribe, in keeping with the well-known formula 'Everything is forbidden, what is permitted is obligatory'. Prescription related not only to the content, but also to the form and even style of a literary work. In time, the decisions of the censorship authorities took on a 'positive', imperative and aggressive character. They did not limit themselves to the prohibition of particular works, the deletion of names and events from the historical record, etc., but instructed authors precisely what they should write and how. So it was that books perfectly loyal and even positively pro-Soviet in tone were banned simply because the author wrote in a non-traditional manner and in the forms of the *avant-garde*.[35] This is the essential difference between the totalitarian censorship of the Soviet period and Russian censorship before the Revolution, which operated, but for a few exceptions, within the framework of the law (the Statutes on Censorship and the Press).[36]

Of course, pre-revolutionary censorship also pursued paternalist aims. This was particularly a feature in the reign of Nicholas I (in general, censorship practice under the Soviet regime has many similarities to the censorship of that period). However, pre-revolutionary censorship was purely defensive in purpose and was based on the existing press legislation. Soviet censorship, on the other hand, was active and aggressive and controlled not by laws but by secret regulations and instructions. One might note other differences between pre- and post-revolutionary censorship, the most significant of which is that while before the Revolution there had been a slow and painful progress towards the relaxation of censorship (with temporary retreats and renewed toughening of rules and practice), after 1917 it became progressively more severe. From the eighteenth century, a gradual process was in train which would eventually release the printed word from its worst yoke—that of preliminary censorship—and replace it with a relatively more liberal post-publication system, with alleged infringements being decided by a court of law. The process was completed at the beginning of the twentieth century: the practice of judging press offences (after publication—in the courts was established and, despite the expense involved, it was a great step forward. After October 1917 preliminary censorship was fully restored: in this regard Russia went back to the times of Nicholas I. Saltykov-Shchedrin once noted that 'Russian literature came into being by oversight of the authorities'. The statement could be rephrased in relation to the Soviet period: Russian literature, contemporary and past, including the 'classics', could exist only by *order* of the authorities.

One of the unforeseen side-effects of total censorship is the function it acquires—naturally, unplanned by the authorities and the censoring agencies themselves—which I shall call the 'provocative' function. By this is meant the heightened interest provoked by censorship in texts which are placed under the ban and forcibly removed from open public access. That such interest should be aroused is entirely understandable and accords with the proverbial truth that goes back to *Genesis*— 'forbidden fruit tastes sweetest'. The devotee of forbidden books has long been familiar. Prince P. A. Vyazemsky recalls a book-lover of Pushkin's time who, whenever his host offered him something to read, always enquired: 'Is it a forbidden book?', and, if the reply was negative, turned it down, adding: 'Very well, I'll wait till you've got something forbidden.' Vyazemsky comments: 'This consumer of uncensored merchandise has the backing of a host of readers. Who has not encountered them? It matters nothing to them if the contraband is good or bad. For them the main attraction is simply that it is contraband.'[37]

This type of reader is perennial. In the Brezhnev years of 'stagnation', when there was an unprecedented circulation of *tamizdat* (Russian books published abroad) and *samizdat* (unofficial home-produced publications), it was quite common to meet such readers, who did not mind what they read provided it was not officially approved and was in one way or another forbidden. There is the story of a girl in her tenth year at school who was 'doing' *War and Peace* in the school syllabus. In all seriousness, she asked her grandmother to make a typed copy of the entire four volumes of the novel, because she was so accustomed to reading *samizdat* that she no longer acknowledged books which were not in that form. Just an anecdote, of course, but highly instructive! Extreme cases apart, the provocative effect of forbidding texts was still very great. Rumours that a book or article was banned created widespread interest in it. Such texts were copied in large numbers by various means, usually the typewriter. At that time it was the dream of every Soviet intellectual to light upon a copy of the *Glavlit* lists of forbidden books. And, although such books were confined to the special collections, sometimes it was possible to find the texts in the back-numbers of journals where they were first published and which were still available in the open sections of a library. A provocative lead was also given by critical articles condemning works as ideologically unsound—interest in such works invariably increased. The enlightened Soviet intellectual assumed that the more a book was damned, the better it must be (by no means always the case, in fact). As a result, critical articles of this kind had a reverse effect, serving as an advertisement for the work condemned. The art-historian I. Tsimbal, who had been introduced in 1960 to the work of the half-banned poet Nikolay Glazkov through a damning article on him in *Izvestiya*, justly remarked: 'one day it will be possible to evaluate the cultural-educational role of those fulminating articles and reviews, without which the intellectual horizons of my generation would then have been far narrower.'[38]

Finally, the last question to be considered is: what were the true causes of the exceptionally harsh censorship operated by the Soviet regime and what were the consequences of its destructive activity during almost three-quarters of the twentieth century?

A great number of the archive documents that I have examined tend to create an impression of absurd surrealism. The pettiness and pathological captiousness displayed by the *Glavlit* officials were, very often, not in the least activated by any possible 'danger' posed by a text totally lacking in subversive intent. But that is the whole point: totalitarian censorship makes no distinction between the important and the unimportant, the material and the immaterial. It seizes equally on a 'criminal', anti-Soviet text and on a trivial misprint in a cross-word or an odd turn of phrase in a translation. The main purpose is to instil terror in anyone who writes, to create general fear and uncertainty in authors who, for their own self-preservation, vainly try to guess at the almost daily changing wishes of the authorities. It is evident that the determining feature of totalitarian censorship is that for it *the fact itself of banning is more important than the contents of the work banned*. In other words, in the totalitarian view repression as such (true also in respect of the physical liquidation of people) has its own self-fulfilling value.

There is another explanation for the extreme severity of the censorship's actions which seem, at first sight, to have been both senseless and inadequate. In Russia, a rigorous and punctilious attitude towards the written and, particularly, the printed word had been pre-determined by the traditional paternalism of the country. The authorities took a deadly serious view of writing—'deadly' in the metaphorical sense, but also in the literal sense, since for writing, or even for reading, a particular book they could put a person to death or at least subject him to severe penalties. The humorous aphorism of Koz′ma Prutkov, 'Many people are like sausages: the filling they are given they carry within them',[39] was viewed by the authorities without a trace of humour. It may be that the collective authors of Koz′ma Prutkov's celebrated works were parodying the vulgar-materialist views of those authors, very popular with the radically minded youth of the 1850s–1860s, whose materialism led them to assert, with Feuerbach, that 'A man is what he eats'. Bolshevik ideologists, whose roots go back to that time, might have offered the paraphrase, 'A man is what he reads'. The logical conclusion of this was that, if that was so, then extraordinary measures must be taken to ensure that a man consumed only such spiritual food as was 'wholesome' (in the eyes of the regime, that is).

The question of how far the regime and its censorship succeeded in its aims is difficult to answer in simple terms. On the one hand, the regime recklessly wasted its potential by conducting a senseless struggle against the reader. Osip Mandel′shtam expressed the view that only Russia has a true love of poetry, because they kill people for it there. And if they don't actually kill, other severe measures are available. In his ice-bound labour-camp Varlam Shalamov, author of the powerful *Stories of Kolyma*, was given a second term in the camp merely for saying in an unguarded moment that Bunin was 'a great Russian writer'.[40] In general, we still know little of the history of resistance to the totalitarian regime—not only of the active resistance, but of the purely intellectual resistance, especially the silent resistance manifested in the seemingly peaceful and innocent matter of choosing, in Soviet conditions, what books to read. The regime's hounding of ideas by the Orwellian 'Thought Police' backfired and in some measure became one of the reasons for its demise. It might be said that the introduction of totalitarian censorship, extreme in its severity, was a kind of subconscious death-wish.

In the outcome, victory went to the reader. Russian literature, in particular the classics, took its revenge by saving the 'Soviet people' (many of them, at least) from being converted into brutes and willing slaves. The regime's policy of playing the 'classics' card, which began in the 1930s when it declared itself heir to the culture of the past, seemed harmless enough. But it had a powerful and unforeseen effect.

M. Kuraev, writing in the 1990s, described the influence of access to the classics on the public as 'an astonishing cultural-historical phenomenon'. Declaring itself heir to the cultural treasures of the nation and permitting the classics to be read in schools and by the public at large, 'the regime, hostile to humanism and justice, found itself defenceless before the—as it turned out—uncontrollable force of the "weapon" [which it had adopted]. The humanist tradition in national culture, in the literature of the nineteenth century, proved to be an insuperable obstacle to the ideology of totalitarianism.'[41] The author is right, though what he says shows clear signs of the Russian tradition of venerating (and exaggerating) the power of the invincible, all-conquering Word, the literary Word in particular: the causes of the collapse of the regime are, of course, more complicated. And it should be remembered that the appropriation of the classical heritage was always under severe ideological control and its products dispensed in strictly rationed doses.

Yet, one must not—as is sometimes done—underestimate the sad and sinister consequences of the censorship terror. More than once in the 1990s we have heard nostalgic laments for the censorship, particularly from former literary functionaries—authors and officials—who were deployed by the communist authorities. It turns out that censorship in no way hindered their 'creative work' and, indeed, even played a certain positive role by preventing the publication of illiterate and 'morally harmful' works. There is also a more 'scientific', if that is the term, justification for censorship and its claimed benign effect on the literary process. It works on a curious analogy: physiologists have observed that a deficiency in one sense or organ can be compensated by the higher development of another—for instance, a person who has lost his hearing may develop improved vision, and vice versa. Similarly, according to some, censorship has the effect—diagnostically indefinable—of causing 'deaf' writers to develop sharper 'vision', that is, to exploit more fully the semantic nuances of words, increase the depth of the sub-text, use the full range of euphemisms, allusions, allegories, etc. But it must be questioned if it is worthwhile depriving a man of his sight in order to improve his hearing. Among other benefits attributed to censorship is the introduction of printing to Russia in the sixteenth century, when it was adopted by the ecclesiastical authorities to produce standardized versions of religious texts, purged of the accumulated errors contained in manuscripts. Even the harsh censorship regime of Nicholas I's reign had a beneficial side-effect in the obligation imposed in 1837 to supply gratis a copy of every book published in Russia to the major public libraries.[42]

For reasons purely of control and fiscal interest the Bolsheviks also, in 1920, adopted the law requiring the deposit of books in the principal libraries, which did, indeed, guarantee that their collections were complete (today this law no longer operates and there are already large gaps in library collections). There is the further, in my view speculative, argument put forward by those who ask: what difference did it really make, in artistic or any other terms, that in Gogol´'s 'Nos' the scene of Major Kovalev's encounter with his nose was switched from the Kazan´ Cathedral (where it took place in the original version) to the Gostinyi dvor? And anyway were not the greatest works of Russian nineteenth-century literature produced in the harsh conditions of censorship then obtaining? These supporters of censorship come round inevitably to the view, once fashionable in *narodnik* circles, that 'the darker the night, the brighter the stars'. They put forward a further and, for them, indisputable argument: 'Look,' they say, 'in the unprecedentedly harsh conditions of total censorship that prevailed in Soviet times major authors were producing their works [they mention the names of Mandel´shtam, Bulgakov, Platonov, Zoshchenko, and, from the period of 'stagnation', Yury Trifonov, Bulat Okudzhava, Fazil´ Iskander, and others], while now, ten years after the virtual abolition of censorship at the end of the 1980s, there is no sign of any new flowering of literature....' What can one say in reply? First, that these major works of literature appeared not because of censorship, but in spite of it; besides which, the pro-censorship view tends to overlook the fact that many authors' greatest works (those of Pushkin, Lermontov, and others) could not be published in their lifetime and appeared only decades later. I will avoid mention of the maimed and shattered lives of writers in Soviet times, many of whom were physically liquidated in the years of the Great Terror. Was the price not too high? Those who support the censorship are experimenting with history, adopting the approach of 'what would have happened, but for...'. I think that if there had been no censorship, Russian literature would not have been the poorer. As for the second point—the absence of any new flowering of literature after the proclamation of *glasnost´* and the abolition of censorship—we are concerned here with an inexplicable phenomenon: geniuses and writers of talent are not born every day and their lives are not bound to coincide with a time when the social-political situation is most favourable.

It is perfectly clear that for seventy years of the twentieth century the totalitarian censorship played a malign role in the historical drama of Russia, bringing about a sharp decline in the spiritual and intellectual potential of the country; the consequences will be felt for years to come. In an essay on the prose works of Marina Tsvetaeva Joseph Brodsky wrote: 'Theoretically, the dignity of a nation degraded politically cannot be seriously wounded by obliterating its cultural heritage. Russia, however, in contrast to nations blessed with a legislative tradition, elected institutions, and so forth, is in a position to understand herself only through literature, and to retard the literary process by disposing of or treating as nonexistent the works of even a minor author is tantamount to a genetic crime against the future of the nation.'[43]

The great English poet and thinker of the seventeenth century, John Milton, declared: 'as good almost to kill a Man as to kill a good Book',[44] a view echoed two centuries later by Heinrich Heine when he wrote that

>...dort wo man Bücher
>Verbrennt, verbrennt man auch am Ende Menschen.[45]

And that is what happened: such is the sad logic of history.

Notes

1. V. Nabokov, *The Gift*, translated by Michael Scammel with the collaboration of the author (London, 1963), 251.
2. For a recent and extensive bibliography, see M. V. Zelenov and M. Dewhirst, 'A Selected Bibliography of Recent Works on Russian and Soviet Censorship', *Solanus* N.S. 11 (1997), 90–8. The section 'Works by Russian authors on the history of Soviet censorship 1988–1995' lists some eighty publications. See also the important compilation *Istoriya sovetskoi politicheskoi tsenzury: Dokumenty i kommentarii*, comp. and ed. T. M. Goryaeva (Moscow, 1997). The present author has published two books on the subject: *Za kulisami "Ministerstva pravdy": tainaya istoriya sovetskoi tsenzury, 1927–1929* (St Petersburg, 1994) and *Sovetskaya tsenzura v epokhu total' nogo terrora, 1929–1953* (St Petersburg, 2000), a collection of documents: *Istoriya sovetskoi tsenzury: Sbornik dokumentov* (Bochum, 1999), and over 30 articles in different journals.
3. *Glavnoe upravlenie po delam literatury i izdatel' stv (Glavlit RSFSR)* was established on 6 June 1922. The abbreviated title *Glavlit* continued in use, despite changes in the designation of the institution: in 1931 it was renamed *Glavnoe upravlenie po okhrane voennykh tain v pechati* and in 1960 *Glavnoe upravlenie po okhrane gosudarstvennykh tain v pechati*. In the late 1980s, during the period of *perestroika*, it was called *Guot* (i.e. *Glavnoe upravlenie po okhrane...tain*). The institution ceased to exist in 1991 when the Press Law of that year declared the abolition of censorship (this was confirmed in the 1993 Constitution of the Russian Federation). See A. V. Blyum, *Sovetskaya tsenzura v epokhu total' nogo terrora, 1929–1953* (St Petersburg, 2000).
4. 'Psycho-Analysis', *The Standard Edition of the Complete Psychological Works of Sigmund Freud*, translated from the German under the General Editorship of James Strachey, xx (London, 1978), 267.
5. Letter to W. Fliess, 22 Dec. 1897, *The Complete Letters of Sigmund Freud to Wilhelm Fliess*, translated and edited by Jeffrey Moussaieff Masson (Cambridge, MA and London, 1985), 289.
6. The phrase is used in *Vo ves' golos*, V. V. Mayakovsky, *Izbrannye proizvedeniya* (Moscow-Leningrad, 1963), ii. 546.
7. E. Dobrenko, *Formovka sovetskogo pisatelya: Sotsial' nye i esteticheskie istoki sovetskoi literaturnoi kul' tury* (St Petersburg, 1999), 12–13.
8. A. Akhmatova, *Stikhotvoreniya i poemy* (Leningrad, 1977), 166.
9. N. Ya. Mandel'shtam, *Vtoraya kniga* (Moscow, 1990), 101.
10. Aleksandr Konstantinovich Voronsky (1883–1943) was a literary critic and from 1921 to 1927 editor-in-chief of the 'fellow-traveller' journal *Krasnaya nov'*. He was expelled from the Communist Party in 1928 and repressed in 1937 (he died in a prison camp in 1943). See A. S. Nezhivoi, *Aleksandr Voronsky—kritik* (Ufa, 1983); (no author), 'Literaturnaya deyatel' nost' A. K. Voronskogo. Materialy nauchnoi konferentsii', *Voprosy literatury* (1985 no. 2), pp. 78–104.
11. The Leningrad division of the children's publishing house Detizdat was established in 1927 under the direction of the writer S. Ya. Marshak. The 'Marshak group' was broken up in 1937–38. Those repressed included the writers S. K. Bezborodov (1903–37, shot), G. G. Belykh (1903–38), N. I. Spiridonov, pseudonym 'Tekki Odulok' (1906–38, died in a prison camp), M. P.

Bronshtein, theoretical physicist and author of popular childrens' books (arrested August 1937, shot February 1938), R. R. Vasil'evna (1902–38, shot); of the editorial staff T. G. Gabbe (1903–60), A. I. Lyubarskaya (1908–), and Z. M. Zadunaiskaya (1903–83) were arrested and many others were dismissed, including Lidiya Chukovskaya, the wife of M. P. Bronshtein. See L. Chukovskaya, *Zapiski ob Anne Akhmatovoi,* i (Moscow, 1989), 240–1, 256; eadem, *V laboratorii redaktora* (Moscow, 1963); A. I. Lyubarskaya, 'Za gran'yu proshlykh dnei. Zametki o Marshake i ego redaktsii', *Neva* (1995 no. 2), 162–70; eadem, 'Za tyuremnoi stenoi', *Neva* (1998 no. 5), 148–72; *Leningradskii martirolog: Kniga pamyati zhertv politicheskikh repressii,* iii: *Noyabr' 1937* (St Petersburg, 1998), index of names.

12. On Tvardovsky as editor of *Novyi mir* in the 1950s-1960s and his colleagues, see A. I. Kondratovich, 'Rovesnik lyubomu pokoleniyu': *Dokumental'naya povest' o Tvardovskom* (Moscow, 1987) and V. Ya. Lakshin, 'Novyi mir' vo vremena Khrushcheva (Moscow, 1991).

13. The 'reader-friend'—the familiar and sympathetic reader, capable of understanding the sub-text of a work—was first identified by the satirist M. E. Saltykov-Shchedrin (1826–89), a noted master of the art of censorship evasion. See his sketch 'Chitatel'' in the cycle *Melochi zhizni* (M. E. Saltykov-Shchedrin, *Polnoe sobranie sochinenii* (Moscow, 1965–77), xvi(2), 133–54).

14. Yu. Trifonov, 'Zapiski soseda', *Druzhba narodov* (1989 no. 11), 36.

15. 'Journal censorship' operated most consistently in the 1960s-1980s in the liberal journals *Novyi mir* and *Oktyabr'* and the blatantly nationalistic *Nash sovremennik* and *Molodaya gvardiya.*

16. OGPU: *Ob"edinennoe gosudarstvennoe politicheskoe upravlenie* 1923–34 (1922–3 simply GPU); NKVD: *Narodnyi komissariat vnutrennikh del* 1934–43; NKGB: *Narodnyi komissariat gosudarstvennoi bezopasnosti* 1943–6; MGB: *Ministerstvo gosudarstvennoi bezopasnosti* 1946–53; KGB: *Komitet gosudarstvennoi bezopasnosti* 1954–91 (the Fifth Directorate of the KGB, instituted in 1969, was responsible for combating political opposition and suppressing dissidence). The KGB was abolished in 1991, though security organs continued to exist under new names—first as *Agentstvo natsional'noi bezopasnosti,* then from 1995 as *Federal'naya sluzhba bezopasnosti.*

17. See, for example, the expert conclusions published in A. V. Blum (ed.), *Tsenzura v SSSR, 1917–1991* (Bochum, 1999), *passim,* esp. 453–7.

18. See the introduction to Goryaeva, *Istoriya sovetskoi politicheskoi tsenzury* (n. 2), and A. V. Blyum, 'Kak bylo razrusheno "Ministerstvo pravdy": sovetskaya tsenzura epokhi glasnosti i perestroiki (1985–1991)', *Zvezda* (1996 no. 6), 212–22.

19. In 1930 the functions of Agitprop were divided between Agitprop for mass campaigns and Kul'tprop (*Kul'tura i propaganda*) for literature and the arts.

20. From 1956 until 1991 the control of literature and culture in general was exercised by the Ideological Department of the Central Committee of the Communist Party.

21. *Gosizdat RSFSR* was created in 1919 and initially, before the establishment of *Glavlit* in 1922, exercised preliminary censorship control. It was abolished in 1931. *Glavpolitprosvet,* under the directorship of N. K. Krupskaya, operated from 1920 to 1932 and had particular responsibility for purging the public libraries of 'counter-revolutionary' works.

22. See the numerous documents (listed in the index of names) in Goryaeva, *Istoriya sovetskoi politicheskoi tsenzury* (n. 2); D. L. Babichenko, *Pisateli i tsenzory: Sovetskaya literatura 1940-kh godov pod politicheskim kontrolem TsK* (Moscow, 1994); idem (ed.), *'Schast'e literatury': Gosudarstvo i pisateli, 1925–1938. Dokumenty* (Moscow, 1997); A. Artizov, O. Naumov (comp.), *Vlast' i khudozhestvennaya intelligentsiya: Dokumenty TsK RKP(b)–VKP(b), VChK–OGPU–NKVD o kul'turnoi politike,1927–1953* (Moscow, 1999).
23. Notable among these were orthodox soviet critics such as V. V. Ermilov (1904–65), V. Ya. Kirpotin (1898–1987), Ya. E. El'sberg (1901–76).
24. J. Brooks, *Thank You, Comrade Stalin!: Soviet Public Culture from Revolution to Cold War* (Princeton, 1999), 247.
25. See also the account of this alternating process in A. Besançon, *Russkoe proshloe i sovetskoe nastoyashchee* (London, 1984), 249.
26. F. M. Dostoevsky, *Polnoe sobranie sochinenii*, iv (Leningrad, 1972), 22.
27. A. I. Solzhenitsyn, *Rossiya v obvale* (Moscow, 1998), 170.
28. See P. N. Medvedeva, *Formalizm i formalisty* (Leningrad, 1934); L. Maksimenkov, *'Sumbur vmesto muzyki': Stalinskaya kul' turnaya revolyutsiya, 1936–1938* (Moscow, 1997); A. V. Blyum, 'Diskussiya o formalizme 1936 g. glazami i ushami stukachei. (Po sekretnym doneseniyam agentov gosbezopasnosti)', *Zvezda* (1996 no. 8), 218–28.
29. See D. L. Babichenko (ed.), *'Literaturnyi front': Istoriya politicheskoi tsenzury, 1832–1946* (Moscow, 1994), 191–239.
30. For details, see A. V. Blyum, 'Khudozhnik i vlast': 12 tsenzurnykh istorii (K 100-letiyu M. M. Zoshchenko)', *Zvezda* (1994 no. 8), 81–91.
31. See L. K. Chukovskaya, *Zapiski ob Anne Akhmatovoi* (Moscow, 1997), ii. 157.
32. On Voronsky, see n. 10 above; for Nikolai Semenovich Angarsky (Klestov) (1873–1943), literary critic and prominent Party activist, see 'Arkhiv N. S. Angarskogo', *Zapiski Otdela rukopisei Gosudarstvennoi biblioteki im. Lenina*, vyp. xxviii (1966), 4–32.
33. George Orwell, *Nineteen Eighty-Four* (Harmondsworth, 2000), 29, 36–7.
34. Vladimir Nabokov, *Lectures on Russian Literature*, ed. Fredson Bowers (London, 1982), 2–3.
35. The works of many *avant-garde* writers (K. Vaginov, V. Khlebnikov, OBERIUT authors such as N. Oleinikov and D. Kharms) were systematically banned on 'aesthetic' rather than political grounds. From 1937 there was also systematic banning of clearly pro-Soviet books whose authors had been repressed and therefore consigned to oblivion.
36. The censorship regulations were laid down in three successive Statutes, promulgated in 1804, 1826 and 1828. The latter, substantially revised in 1865 and 1905–6, remained in force until 1917. For the history and operation of tsarist censorship, see: A. Skabichevsky, *Ocherki istorii russkoi tsenzury (1700–1863 g.)* (St Petersburg, 1892); M. K. Lemke, *Nikolaevskie zhandarmy i literatura, 1826–1855 gg.*, (2nd ed. St Petersburg, 1909); idem, *Epokha tsenzurnykh reform* (St Petersburg, 1904); K. K. Arsen'ev, *Zakonodatel' stvo o pechati* (St Petersburg, 1903); V. Rozenberg, V. Yakushkin, *Russkaya pechat' i tsenzura v proshlom i nastoyashchem: Stat' i* (Moscow, 1905); major studies in English are: Charles A. Ruud, *Fighting Words: Imperial Censorship and the Russian Press, 1804–1906* (Toronto, 1982), Daniel

Balmuth, *Censorship in Russia, 1865–1905* (Washington DC, 1979), and (on the foreign censorship) Marianna Tax Choldin, *A Fence around the Empire: Russian Censorship of Western Ideas under the Tsars* (Durham NC, 1985).

37. P. A. Vyazemsky, *Polnoe sobranie sochinenii* (St Petersburg, 1878–96), viii. 245.
38. I. Tsimbal, 'Odinokii litsedei', *Zvezda* (1999 no. 2), 149.
39. In 'Mysli i aforizmy': Koz'ma Prutkov, *Polnoe sobranie sochinenii* (Moscow-Leningrad, 1965), 131.
40. V. T. Shalamov, *Neskol' ko moikh zhiznei: Proza. Poeziya. Esse* (Moscow, 1996), 7.

Ivan Bunin, the first Russian writer to receive the Nobel Prize for Literature (1933), had emigrated to France in 1920 and was regarded by the Soviet authorities as a renegade.

41. M. Kuraev, 'Zhil-byl chitatel'', *Literaturnaya gazeta*, 1 Mar. 1995, p. 3.
42. See V. I. Kharlamov, 'Tsenzura v kontekste russkoi kul'tury: neissledovannyi aspekt', in *Tsenzura v tsarskoi Rossii i Sovetskom soyuze: Materialy konferentsii 24–27 maya 1993 g.* (Moscow, 1995), 88.
43. Joseph Brodsky, 'A Poet and Prose', in idem, *Less Than One: Selected Essays* (Harmondsworth, 1987), 193.
44. *Areopagitica*, in *Complete Prose Works of John Milton*, ii (New Haven, 1959), 492.
45. 'Where they burn books, in the end they burn people too.' H. Heine, *Historisch-Kritische Gesamtausgabe der Werke*, ed. M. Windfuhr, v (Hamburg, 1994), 16.

Z658.S65 B5817 2003

Blium, A. V. (Arlen
 Viktorovich)
A self-administered
 poison : the system and
    2003.

2006 02 24

0 1341 0839860 0

DISCARD